LOVE

THE CASE FOR

THE FIGHT FOR INTERRACIAL MARRIAGE

BY **SELINA ALKO**

ILLUSTRATED BY **SEAN QUALLS**

AND **SELINA ALKO**

ARTHUR A. LEVINE BOOKS • AN IMPRINT OF SCHOLASTIC INC.

LOVING

Congress Cataloging-in-Publication Data ♥ Alko, Selina. ♥ The case for loving : the fight for interracial marriage / by Selina Alko ; illustrated by Sean Qualls and Selina
Alko.—First Edition.   pages   cm   ♥ Audience: K to Grade 3. ♥ Includes bibliographical references. ♥ ISBN 978-0-545-47853-3 (jacketed hardcover : alk. paper)
1.   Interracial marriage—Juvenile literature.   I. Qualls, Sean, illustrator. II. Alko, Selina, illustrator. III. Title.   ♥   HQ1031.A45 2015 ♥ 306.84′6—dc23
♥ 2014005329 ♥ 10 9 8 7 6 5 4 3 2 1   15 16 17 18 19 ♥ Printed in Malaysia   108 ♥ First printing, January 2015 ♥ The text type was set in Adobe Garamond
Bold Pro. ♥ The display type was set in Bad Typ. ♥ The illustrations were created using mixed media: paint (gouache and acrylic), collage, and colored pencil on bristol board. ♥
Art direction and book design by Marijka Kostiw ♥

TO ISAIAH AND GINGER,
WITH ALL OUR LOVE.

AND SPECIAL THANKS
TO REBECCA SHERMAN.

—SELINA & SEAN

FIRST COMES LOVE.
THEN COMES
MARRIAGE.

Donald, Peggy, and Sidney had two parents who loved
them, and who loved each other.

In fact, from almost the moment Richard Loving met
Mildred Jeter they wanted to get married and have a family.

But for them, it wasn't that simple, and here's why:

Richard was white: a fair-skinned boy who got quickly sunburned in July. Mildred was what they called "colored" in those days: her skin a creamy caramel.

In 1958, they lived in the small town of Central Point, Virginia, where people every shade from the color of chamomile tea to summer midnight made their homes.

Richard Loving was a good, caring man; he didn't see differences. There was one person Richard loved more than the rest. Mildred Jeter was part African-American, part Cherokee, but what most folks in Central Point noticed was how thin she was; that's how she got the nickname, "String Bean."

When Richard popped the question,
String Bean jumped with joy!

The two were in love; they felt it should be their right to get married.
Sadly, it was not.

Not in Virginia or sixteen other states. In those places, marriage between people of different races was against the law!

WHITE

A hundred years earlier, slavery divided America along color lines.
   Even after slavery ended, some white people weren't used to blacks being free, let alone free to marry whom they chose.
   If you married someone who had skin color unlike your own, you could go to jail!

   Mildred and Richard wanted to get married,
but they did not want to spend any time in prison.

COLORED

Although they couldn't have a legal marriage in Virginia, they could right next door in Washington, D.C. So they invited a few friends and family to witness their wedding across state lines.

At the ceremony, nobody objected when Richard said, "I do," and Mildred said, "I do," too.

The Lovings were officially pronounced husband and wife!
The blushing bride and her groom smiled all the way from D.C.
back to their house in Virginia.

They couldn't wait to start a family!

But soon, something terrible happened. In the middle
of the night, they were awoken from their sleep.

It was the police!

An officer shouted at Richard, "What are you doing
with that woman?"

Richard proudly pointed to their marriage certificate
(hanging on the wall).

"That's not good here!" the policeman boomed.

And just like that, Mildred and Richard were taken away and locked up in jail. They were charged with "unlawful cohabitation," which means living together against the law. The Lovings didn't think there was anything unlawful about their love at all. If anything, the way they were treated should have been unlawful!

IT WAS JUST AWFUL!

UNLAWFUL

COHABITATION

After a few nights behind bars, Richard and Mildred were told they had to leave Virginia if they wanted to live together as

MR. AND MRS. LOVING.

So with heavy hearts, the pair hugged their families,
packed their bags, and left their home.

They tried to make a life for themselves in D.C. Richard found a job
laying bricks, and String Bean gave birth to three babies, three different shades
of milk-chocolate brown.

DONALD, PEGGY, AND SIDNEY.

But the city didn't suit the Lovings.
There were too many cars!
There was too much concrete!
They missed Central Point with its rolling hills and open spaces. They missed
their friends and families. They missed their home.

They wanted to return to Virginia for good, so they hired lawyers to help fight for what was right.

**BY NOW iT WAS 1966,
AND THE TiMES
THEY WERE A-CHANGiN'.**

Brand-new ideas, like equal rights for people of all colors,
were replacing old, fearful ways of thinking.

VOTI
RIGH

JOBS
NOW

END
SEGREGATED
SCHOOLS

NO
JIM
CROW

POLICE
ROR
UST
CO

EFOM

The lawyers worked around the clock to make the case for interracial marriage as strong as possible.

IT WAS TIME TO TAKE THE LOVING CASE ALL THE WAY TO THE SUPREME COURT!

· EQUAL · JUSTICE · UNDER · LAW ·

On June 12, 1967, when the case of *Loving v. Virginia* began, Richard and Mildred stayed at home with Donald, Peggy, and Sidney. They were all nervous and afraid they would not win.

The state argued that in order to preserve the "purity of the white race," blacks and whites must remain separate!

Then it was the Lovings' lawyers' turn to present their case. They said it was UNCONSTITUTIONAL to make marriage a crime because of race.

"tell the court

And they read a message from Richard himself:

"TELL THE COURT I LOVE MY WIFE, AND IT IS JUST UNFAIR THAT I CAN'T LIVE WITH HER IN VIRGINIA."

It didn't take long for a decision to be made.
It was unanimous: The court ruled in favor of the Lovings!
Interracial couples could now legally marry in Virginia.
Richard and Mildred hugged. They won the right to their love.

THEY WERE
FREE AT LAST.

Over nine years after their arrest, the Lovings packed their bags one final time. Richard planned to build a big, roomy brick house in Central Point. String Bean was ready to start their life over.

The Loving family returned to Virginia to live.

HAPPiLY (AND LEGALLY!) EVER AFTER.

AUTHOR'S NOTE BY SELINA ALKO

My husband, Sean Qualls, and I were first introduced at a wedding because of all we had in common, particularly that we were both illustrators. We fell in love and were married in New York in 2003 with great ease and acceptance. I happen to be a white Jewish woman from Canada, and Sean is an African-American man from New Jersey. So much of our lives and so much of my work is about inclusion and diversity. I must admit, it's difficult to imagine that just decades ago couples just like us not only faced discrimination, but were told by their governments that their love was unlawful.

The Loving family
PHOTO: GREY VILLET © ESTATE OF GREY VILLET

Sean Qualls and Selina Alko
PHOTO: TED LEWIS 2013

In our home, like any home across the country and around the world, we tell our children, Isaiah and Ginger, stories from our childhood, about our parents and grandparents. These are tales of their personal history, but in a way, so is the story of Richard Loving and Mildred Jeter.

To today's children, it may seem unbelievable that women were not always granted the right to vote, there was a time when African-Americans did not have the same freedoms as white people, and that people of different racial and ethnic backgrounds were not legally allowed to marry.

With twenty-first-century eyes, it is shocking that the state of Virginia would criminalize the Lovings' union. In 1967, when the Lovings took their case to court, Virginia was one of five states that banned interracial marriage. Today every state legalizes interracial marriage, but the fight for equality continues. When I first wrote this manuscript in 2011, only five states legalized same-sex marriage. As of today in early 2014, there are seventeen states wherein gay marriage is legal.

It is our hope that there will soon come a time when all people who love each other have the same rights as Sean and I have.

ABOUT THE ART

For years, Sean and I have thought about illustrating a book together; we were just waiting for the right story to come along. Once I wrote *The Case for Loving* manuscript, it seemed the natural choice.

We both use paint and collage, which gave us a foundation for blending our styles together. But where Sean tends to be more introspective and emotional (taking his time to create subtle layers of color and texture), I am more spontaneous and burst forth with bold color.

Just like a marriage is the joining of two people, the illustrations for this book could not be achieved individually, but only by Sean and me working together.

Sources

"The Crime of Being Married. A Virginia couple fights to overturn an old law against miscegenation."
Photographs by Grey Villet, *Life Magazine*, March 18, 1966.

Alonso, Karen. *Loving v. Virginia: Interracial Marriage*. Berkeley Heights, NJ: Enslow Publishers, 2000.

Dominus, Susan. "The Color of Love." *New York Times Magazine*. December 23, 2008.

May It Please the Court: Transcripts of 23 Live Recordings of Landmark Cases as Argued Before the Supreme Court. Ed. Peter Irons and Stephanie Guitton. New York: The New Press, 1994.

Newbeck, Phyl. *Virginia Hasn't Always Been for Lovers: Interracial Marriage Bans and the Case of Richard and Mildred Loving*. Carbondale, IL: Southern Illinois University Press, 2004.

Sheppard, Kate. "The Loving Story: How an Interracial Couple Changed a Nation." Rev. of *The Loving Story*, directed by Nancy Buirski, motherjones. com. February 13, 2012. Web.

The Loving Story. Directed by Nancy Buirski. HBO Documentary Films, 2012. DVD.

The Loving Story: Photographs by Grey Villet. January 20–May 6, 2012. Photography exhibit, International Center of Photography, New York.

Villet, Barbara. "The Heart of the Matter: Love." *The New York Times Lens Blog. New York Times*, January 16, 2012. Web.

Villet, Grey. "Love Supreme: An Interracial Romance Triumphs in 1960s Virginia," *Life.com*. Web.

Suggestions for Further Reading

Adoff, Arnold. *Black Is Brown Is Tan*. Illus. Emily Arnold McCully, New York: HarperCollins, 1973.

McBride, James. *The Color of Water: A Black Man's Tribute to His White Mother*. New York: Riverhead Books, 1996.

Pinkney, Andrea Davis. *Sit-In: How Four Friends Stood Up by Sitting Down*. Illus. Brian Pinkney, New York: Little, Brown Books for Young Readers, 2010.

Rappaport, Doreen. *Martin's Big Words: The Life of Martin Luther King, Jr.* Illus. Brian Collier, New York: Hyperion Books for Children, 2001.

Shelton, Paula Young. *Child of the Civil Rights Movement*. Illus. Raul Colón, New York: Schwartz & Wade, an imprint of Random House, Inc., 2010.

To Tiffany and Nicholas

—C.C.

To Jon Byron, the pages of your life shine with the radiance of God.

—J.B.

Harper Blessings
HarperCollins Publishers

The Twelve Prayers of Christmas
Text copyright © 2009 by Candy Chand Illustrations copyright © 2009 by James Bernardin
Manufactured in China. All rights reserved. No part of this book may be used or reproduced
in any manner whatsoever without written permission except in the case of brief quotations
embodied in critical articles and reviews. For information address HarperCollins Children's Books,
a division of HarperCollins Publishers, 10 East 53rd Street, New York, NY 10022.
www.harpercollinschildrens.com

Library of Congress Cataloging-in-Publication Data
Chand, Candy.
    The twelve prayers of Christmas / by Candy Chand ; illustrated by James Bernardin. —
1st ed.
        p.   cm.
    ISBN 978-0-06-077636-7 (trade bdg) — ISBN 978-0-06-077637-4 (lib bdg)
    1. Jesus Christ—Nativity—Meditations—Juvenile literature. 2. Christian children—
Prayers and devotions. I. Bernardin, James. II. Title.
BT315.3.C43   2009   2008016215
242'.82—dc22   CIP
                                                                            AC

Typography by Jeanne L. Hogle
09 10 11 12 13 SCP 10 9 8 7 6 5 4 3 2 1
❖
First Edition

The Twelve Prayers of Christmas

by Candy Chand

illustrated by James Bernardin

HARPER  BLESSINGS

HarperCollinsPublishers

Mary

My heart's filled with peace.
I know there's a plan.
We'll find our way home
as soon as we can.

For now I'm content
to follow His lead
to Bethlehem's door.
God's voice I will heed.

When my child is born,
the world will know
Earth is His calling,
but Heaven's His home.

The Donkey

I walk with great joy;
I travel with zeal.
I carry God's gift;
no burden I feel.

We wander by day;
we roam through the night.
Our path is assured;
my spirit is light.

There's no need to struggle;
there's no cause for fear.
I was born for this purpose.
His voice do I hear.

We'll arrive right on time,
not a minute too late.
For I'm part of God's plan;
it's my blessed fate.

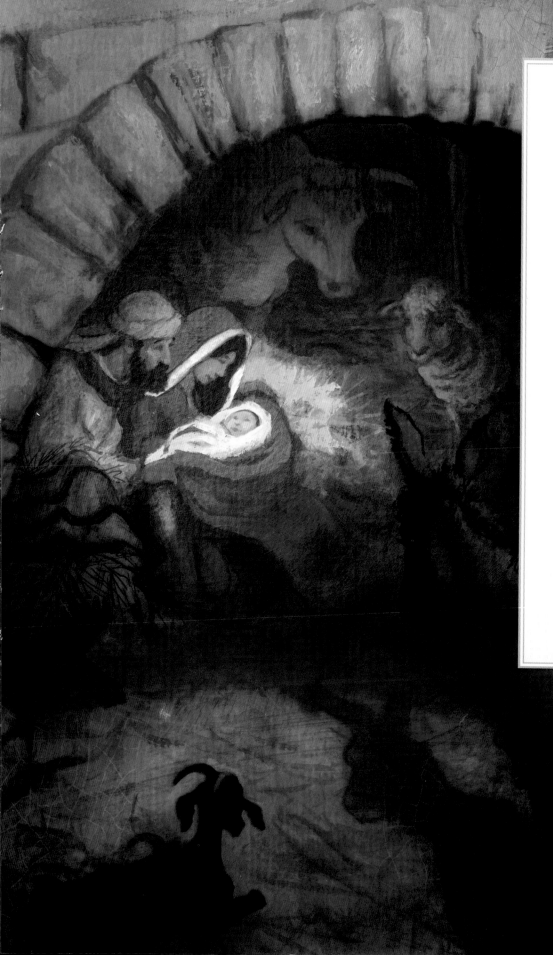

The Innkeeper

I could not have known,
when I turned them away,
pure love from above
would soon lie in the hay.

I could not have known
He would be crowned King,
'til I heard for myself
when the Angels did sing.

I should have known better,
but I know now.
God's Son has been born;
I humbly bow.

Joseph

My wife is now resting;
my babe is asleep.
My heart is rejoicing;
no longer I weep.

In one sacred instant
our lives have been changed.
For the Lord of the Earth
has graced our domain.

Miracles abound.
Angels shout from the sky,
"Messiah is born;
we praise Him on high!"

The Star

For this I burst forth,
my purpose to shine
to light a bright path
to the Savior divine.

To beam down a glow
from Heaven to Earth,
alighting the place
of His Holy birth.

My blaze will burn out
once my mission is done,
when all who must find Him
seek God's only Son.

The First Wise Man

I ride through the desert
in search of a sign.
A babe I will seek;
a King I shall find.

I carry a treasure:
frankincense in a jar,
perfume for my Lord,
a gift from afar.

I'll travel forever,
if that's what it takes,
until my eyes gaze at
His young, Holy face.

The Second Wise Man

I come from the east.
I travel by night,
pursuing a star
in search of the light.

I'll find my true yearning
when I finally see
my purpose to wander,
the reason I breathe.

I'll offer Him myrrh,
a treasure from Earth,
then call Him my Lord,
Messiah by birth.

The Third Wise Man

I'm hungry and tired;
I've roamed 'til I'm weak.
I won't rest 'til I find Him,
this Lord of the meek.

When I finally behold Him,
I shall celebrate.
I'll sing with pure joy.
On Him, I will wait.

I'll offer bright gold;
I'll grant royal praise.
I'll give Him my heart
for the rest of my days.

The Angel

Awake from your dreams;
arise in the night.
Hear my voice;
follow the light.

Do not be afraid;
do not run and hide.
Behold God's gift
to the world tonight.

The moment you find Him,
you'll know what to do:
Bow down in His presence.
My message is true.

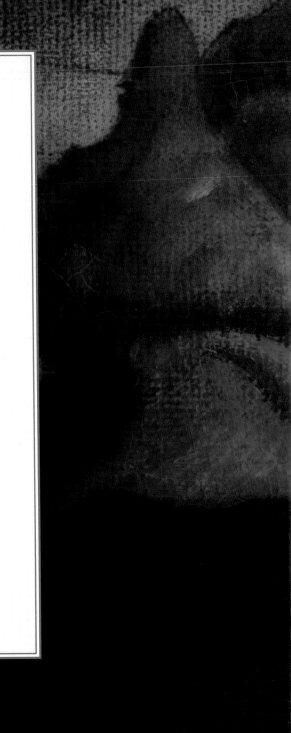

The Shepherd

I am a poor shepherd;
I work by starlight.
I sleep in the valley
on cold, lonely nights.

From this moment on,
I'll not be the same,
for a mighty angel
just whispered my name.

The promise was vivid;
the words were quite clear:
"I bring you great tidings,
young lad, do not fear.

"In the city of David,
at Bethlehem's door,
a Babe in a stable,
ordained Christ the Lord."

I must seek His presence
while angels draw near
to worship this newborn
whom Heaven holds dear.

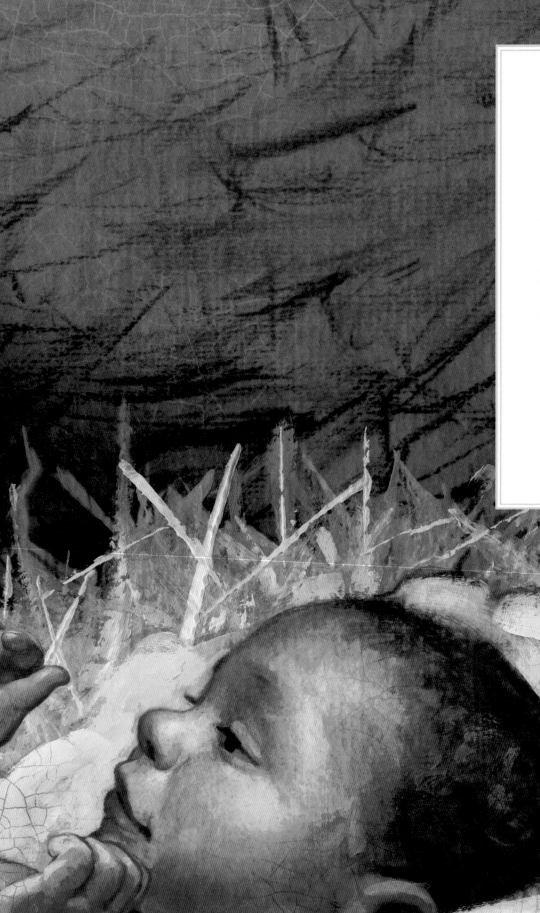

The Lamb

I never imagined
I'd charm royal guests.
I never believed
I'd watch my Lord rest.

But miracles happen—
yes, even to me.
For my humble home
has been graced by a King.

The Christ Child

I was born in a stable,
in a simple abode,
without a gold crown
nor rich, royal robe.

I am the true Savior.
I came to bring peace
for every last person,
from greatest to least.

My message is simple;
my mission is clear.
Listen intently;
you've nothing to fear.

I've come for one purpose:
His will shall be done
when all sense God's heart
in the soul of His Son.